Home Office Research Study 157

Testing obscenity: an international comparison of laws and controls relating to obscene material

by
Sharon Grace

A Research and Statistics Directorate Report

Home Office
Research and
Statistics
Directorate

London: Home Office

Home Office Research Studies

The Home Office Research Studies are reports on research undertaken by or on behalf of the Home Office. They cover the range of subjects for which the Home Secretary has responsibility. Titles in the series are listed at the back of this report (copies are available from the address on the back cover). Other publications produced by the Research and Statistics Directorate include Research Findings, the Research Bulletin, Statistical Bulletins and Statistical Papers.

The Research and Statistics Directorate

The Directorate consists of three Units which deal with research and statistics on Crime and Criminal Justice, Offenders and Corrections, Immigration and General matters; the Programme Development Unit; the Economics Unit; and the Operational Research Unit.

The Research and Statistics Directorate is an integral part of the Home Office, serving the Ministers and the department itself, its services, Parliament and the public through research, development and statistics. Information and knowledge from these sources informs policy development and the management of programmes; their dissemination improves wider public understanding of matters of Home Office concern.

First published 1996

Application for reproduction should be made to the Information and Publications Group, Room 1308, Home Office, Apollo House, 36 Wellesley Road, Croydon CR9 3RR.

©Crown copyright 1996 ISBN 1 85893 672 1
ISSN 0072 6435

Foreword

The aim of the research described in this report was to compare obscenity laws and controls in England and Wales with those in a number of other countries in order to discover the various ways in which countries define and deal with obscenity in printed matter, at the cinema and on video. The various systems used by the different countries are assessed and compared in an attempt to explore the effectiveness of the different approaches for dealing with such material. In particular, the report focuses on the respective merits of proactive and reactive approaches. The research provides a context in which any future discussions of present laws and controls can take place.

CHRISTOPHER NUTTALL
Director of Research and Statistics

Acknowledgements

I would like to thank my colleagues Lee Hughes and Nick Hunt in the Sentencing and Offences Unit for their help in setting up this project and in making the necessary contacts in the participating countries. I would also like to thank Laurie Kelleher and Roderick Macauley at the Crown Prosecution Service for advice and information on the relevant law. Malcolm Ramsay, my colleague in the Research and Statistics Directorate, gave helpful comments on a draft report.

Most importantly, I am very grateful to all the countries who took part in the study and to their representatives who provided both vast quantities of helpful information and constructive comments on a draft report. I am also very grateful to Margaret Ford at the British Board of Film Classification for giving up her time so generously and providing a valuable insight into the workings of her organisation.

SHARON GRACE

Contents

Summary

Introduction

The study described in this report aimed to compare the obscenity laws in England and Wales with those in a number of other countries in order to discover the various ways in which countries define and deal with obscenity in printed material, at the cinema and on video. The different systems used were compared in an attempt to explore the effectiveness of the different approaches.

Seven countries were selected for the review, as well as England and Wales. These were Australia, Canada, New Zealand, Scotland, Germany, The Netherlands and the Republic of Ireland. The relevant literature on the situation in the USA was also reviewed.

Key questions were asked of appropriate officials in each country:

- What legal controls are there for classifying and censoring sexually explicit material?

- Is there an organisation, committee or similar for dealing with the classification and censoring of sexually explicit material?

- What balance is there between proactive and reactive controls of sexually explicit material?

- How are cases involving breaches in the law prosecuted?

- What are the legal tests for defining what is obscene for video, cinema and the written word – if different?

- Is there a system for codifying what is and what is not acceptable or is this defined under case law?

A literature review on twentieth century debates about obscenity was also undertaken.

Key points

General approach

- Countries tend to favour either a predominantly proactive or reactive approach to controlling obscene material. The choice of approach impacts on all legislation concerned with regulating such material.

- Those countries whose legislation focuses on the proactive classification of obscene material tend to have rigid definitions of what is deemed to be obscene which, it can be argued, allows for a more objective and simple assessment of such material.

- The alternative approach enables the definition of obscenity to develop over time, through case law. This is a more complex process which has to take into account perhaps contradictory judgements made over a long period of time. Whilst such a system is necessarily more subjective, it may more easily reflect current (and changing) standards in society.

Cinema

- The majority of countries have some form of classification and/or censorship of films prior to their release at the cinema – some working with the film industry, basing judgements on experience; others within a specific piece of legislation which outlines the criteria upon which their decisions must be made. Again, a flexible approach allows for a judgement to be made about the context in which any image is depicted, so that nothing is ruled out simply on the basis of it being included on an 'outlawed' list. However, it can be difficult, with such a system, to know why a particular film is classified in a particular way. A system which uses written criteria enables one to see more easily why a film is given a certain category but does not so readily allow the context of the narrative to be taken into account.

Video

- In some countries, the viewing of films on video is seen as conceptually different to viewing films at the cinema and, as a result, different criteria are applied when controlling material on video. The reasons for this are that viewing video allows for a more concentrated viewing of images and it is more difficult to prevent children and other vulnerable people seeing inappropriate material in the home.

- Such concerns are reflected in legislation which applies stricter criteria for classifying video. Films have to be re-submitted prior to their release on video and may require cuts and/or receive a different classification (than for the cinema).

Printed material

- Of all the media, the control of obscene printed material appears to be the most difficult and results in the widest variety of arrangements between the countries included in the review. Some countries make no attempt to classify or censor printed material prior to publication. Those that do, tend only to classify those publications that are likely to exceed their obscenity rules. Realistically such systems are unlikely to capture anything like the real market in printed material. However it can be argued that having some form of classification can make the prosecution of such material more straightforward.

Child pornography and child protection

- One of the key purposes for controlling obscenity is to protect young people and this concern is reflected in special legislation in many countries. In most jurisdictions, the mere possession of indecent photographs of children is an offence and penalties are severe. All countries include, in their definitions of obscenities or classifications codes, specific categories concerned with the sexual imagery of children and regardless of the way in which countries control obscene material overall, they all take very seriously the protection of children from such images.

1 Introduction

Background

From the time when printed matter first became widely available, arguments have ensued about what might be contained in such publications and who, if anyone, should have control over their contents. Because of the diversity of opinion on this issue, legislating against alleged infringements of any controls has always been difficult, giving rise to much public debate. The problem became more complex with the advent of cinema and, more recently, video and computers.

The aim of this paper is to compare the laws in England and Wales with those in a number of other countries in order to discover the various ways in which countries define and deal with obscenity in printed material, at the cinema and on video. The various systems used by the different countries are assessed and compared in an attempt to explore the effectiveness of the different approaches for dealing with such material. In particular, the report focuses on the respective merits of proactive and reactive approaches. This international review is prefaced by a discussion of twentieth century debates about obscenity laws (see Chapter Two).

It should be emphasised that this report does not aim to discuss the possible harmful effects of obscene material. In particular, it does not discuss the evidence of links between pornography and sexual violence. These arguments have been fully rehearsed elsewhere (see, for example, Howitt and Cumberbatch, 1990 and Itzin, 1992) and most observers would accept that empirical research has been unsuccessful at either proving or disproving any causal link.[1] Dwyer (1995) effectively summarises the dilemma of using such 'empirical evidence':

> "[I]t is unclear what generalisations can be made about the connection between the consumption of pornography and sexual violence against women ..... Researchers have provided conflicting answers .... Various biases operate in the design of experiments and questionnaires and in the interpretation of their results; the same 'expert testimony' is em-

---

1   Nevertheless, the debate about the possible damaging effect of obscene material is an integral part of any discussion about the ways in which the law defines and deals with such material.

ployed in very different, often opposing, political and pragmatic arguments. Such uncertainty renders problematic the appeal to such research in arguments for either restrictive or permissive policies on pornography."

Selection of countries

Seven countries were selected to be included in the review as well as England and Wales.[2] These were Australia, Canada, New Zealand, Scotland, Germany, The Netherlands and the Republic of Ireland. The first four countries were selected because their legal systems were based on or allied to the British system and thus had a similar starting point to our own with regard to obscenity law. Germany was selected as it has comparable video censorship to our own, although their system is reputed to be more costly and complicated. The Netherlands was chosen to represent what is generally considered to be a more permissive approach to sexually explicit material. Finally, the Republic of Ireland was included because, although it has a similar legal system to our own, its views on censorship are supposed to be heavily influenced by the Catholic Church.

The following questions were asked of appropriate officials in each of these countries:

- What legal controls are there for classifying and censoring sexually explicit material?

- Is there an organisation, committee or similar for dealing with the classification and censoring of sexually explicit material?

- What balance is there between proactive and reactive controls of sexually explicit material?

- How are cases involving breaches in the law prosecuted?

- What are the legal tests for defining what is obscene for video, cinema and the written word, if different?

- Is there a system for codifying what is and what is not acceptable or is this defined under case law?

It was not possible within the timescales of this study to include an empi-

---

2   Any differences between England and Wales and Northern Ireland will also be highlighted.

rical examination of USA laws on obscenity. American laws tend to be state-specific and thus it would have been a huge task to ensure that all state legislation was covered. However, given the strong connection between British and American laws, the American literature on the subject is discussed in some detail.

Structure of report

The various debates and arguments which have developed around the legislation against obscene material, focusing on the twentieth century, are discussed in Chapter Two. Chapter Three reports on the empirical part of the study and covers the responses obtained from the international review and Chapter Four discusses the key characteristics of the different systems. Finally, some overall conclusions about the various approaches are offered in Chapter Five.

2 Twentieth century debates about obscenity laws

The development of twentieth century law

In the first half of the twentieth century, English obscenity laws were predominantly used to prohibit the publication of allegedly obscene *written* material. The Hicklin test still dominated as the key test of obscenity:

> "... whether the tendency of the matter charged as obscenity is to deprave and corrupt those whose minds are open to such immoral influences and into whose hands a publication of this sort might fall." (R v Hicklin 1868 LR 3 QB 360 at 371.)

Early in the century, there was little or no discussion about the possible merits of the books being prosecuted – literary value was irrelevant (Macmillan, 1983). Nor did the whole of the book need to be deemed obscene. Most famously perhaps, in the prosecution of Radclyffe Hall's *The Well of Loneliness* in 1928, a key phrase suggesting lesbian activity "And that night they were not divided" was judged to be obscene and this was sufficient to prohibit the whole text.

As the century moved on, a debate ensued about whether it was the rightful place of the criminal law to define a serious work of literature as obscene (see Newburn, 1992). Parliament finally responded to this debate with the implementation of the Obscene Publications Act (OPA) 1959. The new Act had four key provisions:

> "[T]hat the work will be taken as a whole; that it shall be considered relative to its effect on its likely readers; that a public good defence is available for works deemed to be obscene in fact; and that the mechanism of trial by jury is foregrounded". (Hunter et al. 1993).

In addition, the Act introduced a new definition of obscenity – to replace the Hicklin test:

> "For the purposes of this Act, an article shall be deemed to be obscene if its effect or (where the article comprises two or more distinct items) the effect of any one of its items is, if taken as a whole, such as to tend to deprave and corrupt persons, who are likely having regard to all relevant circumstances, to read, see or hear the matter contained or embodied in

it." (OPA 1959, Section 1 (1).)

In these ways, it was hoped that the new Act would ensure that serious works of literature would be protected from prohibition by the use of a defence of public good and the Act allowed expert evidence to be presented on this point. No longer did one have to consider the impact of the work on the most impressionable teenager (if it was unlikely that such a reader would see the book) nor was it any longer the case that one passage would be sufficient to render the whole publication outlawed.

A year after the implementation of the OPA 1959, Penguin Books Ltd were prosecuted for the publication of D.H. Lawrence's *Lady Chatterley's Lover*. The story of this trial has been fully discussed and documented elsewhere (see, for example, Rolph, 1961; Newburn, 1992; and Hunter et al. 1993) and such discussion will not be repeated here. Suffice to say that the jury returned a verdict of "not guilty"; the significance of which should not be underestimated. Although, as Newburn (1992) rightly points out "the written word was still by no means safe" and written publications would continue to be prosecuted regularly up until the mid 1970s, there was a change in focus away from the prosecution of *written* word for obscenity towards the prosecution of visual imagery and cases against written material are virtually unheard of today.

The development of film censorship[1]

Film censorship in Britain stemmed, rather bizarrely, early this century, from a concern about fire risks in unlicensed buildings opening up as cinemas. In response to such concerns, Parliament passed the 1909 Cinematograph Act which required all buildings showing films to have a licence issued by the local authority. The Act, however, was drafted in rather vague terms and, as a result, designated local authorities as film censors. They remain so to this day.

The film industry's reaction to this legislation was to appeal to the Home Secretary on the grounds that it would be an extremely costly and time consuming business to submit films to all local authorities for approval prior to their release. They made two suggestions to the Home Secretary: that they set up an independent censorship board which would view all films and classify them; and that the Home Office should be the final arbiter in cases of appeal. The Home Secretary agreed to the first proposal but rejected the second. Trevelyan (1978) suggests that the reason for this was that "he was

---

[1]   For a detailed history of film censorship in this country, see Phelps, 1975; Trevelyan, 1978; Brophy, 1977; and, more recently, Mathews, 1995.

reluctant for himself or his Department to be involved in something that might be controversial, a view which has been held by all subsequent Home Secretaries".

Thus the British Board of Film Censors was established[2] in 1912 by the film industry. Early classifications were restricted to approving a film for universal exhibition or indicating that the film was not recommended for children. The system was purely voluntary. In 1923, the Home Office issued model conditions to local authorities which recognised the jurisdiction of the Board:

> "No film – other than photographs of current events – which has not been passed for "universal" or "public" exhibition by the British Board of Films Censors shall be exhibited without the express consent of the Council".

By the mid 1920s it had become general practice for local authorities to accept the decision of the Board, which had, by that time, become independent of the film industry.

Against what should we legislate?

Although, as discussed earlier, prosecutions against the written word are now virtually unknown, arguments continue about what kinds of material should be censored or legislated against. For example, should it be material that is designed solely for the purposes of being pornographic/obscene or, alternatively, material that is, almost by default, obscene or pornographic? In other words, can consideration be given as to what the original intention of the producer or distributor of the material was – to commercially exploit obscenity or to produce a work of art which could be considered by some observers to be obscene?

Although the terms obscene and pornographic are not synonymous in law, it has become more and more the case that, in reality, it is pornography which is legislated against.[3] Most often, when using the term obscene, one is referring to sexually explicit material, but not always. The problems of definition do not stop there. What is, for example, the difference between 'erotica' and 'soft-core' pornography? Or between 'soft-core' and 'hard-core' pornography? And, which of these categories can be defined as obscene? Whilst many people accept that certain categories of pornography should be

---

2   The workings of the present day British Board of Film Classification will be discussed in the next chapter.
3   Indeed, it has been argued that one of the key aims behind the OPA 1959 was to ensure that it was 'pornography' that was prosecuted rather than 'literature' (Dhavan and Davies, 1978)

outlawed – most obviously, those involving children[4] – others would argue that all judgements made about obscene or pornographic material are simply a matter of taste – and how does one legislate for or against certain tastes?

Who is the target audience?

At the other end of the process, the question of the target audience for the material must also be addressed. One of the key factors to consider in obscenity legislation, under the OPA 1959, is whether or not the material has a tendency to deprave or corrupt its *likely* readers. As discussed earlier, it is no longer necessary to assume, as it was under common law, that anyone, including the most vulnerable, is likely to come across the material. This means that the concept of obscenity becomes relative in the legislation – relative to the likely audience for the material (Robertson, 1979). Thus it is accepted that consideration needs to be given to the number, age, taste, maturity, educational level and motivation of any potential audience (Hunter et al. 1993). This also implies that a particular type of material might provoke different reactions in different people – some might be depraved and corrupted and others not. In a trial, the prosecution would therefore have to prove that a significant proportion of those people who would be likely to view or read the material would be depraved and corrupted by it, rather than simply proving that the material is obscene *per se*.

It becomes even more difficult to resolve this matter if the likely audience can be judged to have been depraved and corrupted prior to having seen the material. For example, if a group of paedophiles view child pornography, one could argue that such material cannot be capable of depraving and corrupting what are obviously already a depraved and corrupt group. Alternatively, it could be argued that it is possible to re-deprave and re-corrupt such an audience an infinite number of times. In 1972, the House of Lords stated that the OPA 1959:

> "is not merely concerned with the once-and-for-all corruption of the wholly innocent, it equally protects the less innocent from further corruption, the addict from feeding or increasing his addiction." (DPP v.Whyte [1972] 3 All E.R. 12, at pp24(h), 25(g-j))

Thus, by selling child pornography to an addicted paedophile, a seller can be seen to be contributing to the paedophile's continuing depravity and corruption (Robertson, 1979).

---

4   For an interesting discussion on the current debate about photographing naked children see Newnham and Townsend's article in *The Guardian* January 13, 1996.

An associated argument questions how one can easily demonstrate whether or not someone has been depraved and corrupted by certain obscene material. The law states that one only has to prove a *tendency* to deprave and corrupt but offers little guidance as to how this tendency might manifest itself. Yet again, one is drawn into ideas of relativity - one person's idea of depravity might be quite different from another's.

Eysenck tested notions of depravity by asking a group of people to judge whether certain activities were depraved. He found that:

> "[T]he spectrum of opinion goes right across the board, from one extreme of permissiveness to the other extreme of puritanism without a break anywhere. There is no evidence here of that substratum of reasonable argument on which the law seems to rely." (Eysenck, 1978)

There is no recourse to expert witnesses to assist the jury in making a decision about whether obscene material might deprave and corrupt.[5] Williams (1981) highlighted the ruling made by the House of Lords in the Whyte[6] case:

> "...the words 'deprave and corrupt' refer to the effect on the mind, including the emotions, and [that] it is not necessary that any physical or overt sexual activity should result." (Williams, 1981)

However, it is difficult to see how this renders the judgement about depravity or corruption easier to make.

One of the more curious arguments for not legislating against obscene material suggests that the more grossly offensive an obscene article is, the more likely it is to repulse or repel the reader/viewer. If this is the case, it would logically follow that the more obscene and disgusting an image is, the more likely it is that one would be repelled by that image to such an extent that one would wholly reject it rather than be influenced, and thus depraved and corrupted, by it. This would appear to be particularly valid if the full consequences of the action depicted are shown - i.e. a rapist being punished for his offence.

However, this argument presumes an 'average readership'. It could be argued that it is more likely that those wishing to see, for example, particularly vicious sado-masochistic material, might be already inclined, or willing to become inclined, to such images and therefore would not be repelled or repulsed by them. Thus the 'aversion theory' loses some of its

---

5   In exceptional circumstances expert evidence can be admissible - see DPP v A and B C Chewing Gum Ltd (1968 QB 159 and Archbold Vol 2 31-79).
7   DPP v. Whyte [1972] 3 All E.R. 12, at pp24(h), 25(g-j)

strength (Robertson, 1979).

It has been argued that testing the tendency to deprave and corrupt has, in practice, been replaced by a judgement based on current community standards (Williams, 1981). Thus, the jury (or the magistrate), as representatives of society, still make a judgement about whether the material in question is obscene based on what would be acceptable to "ordinary decent people".[7]

This notion of community standards has had an important impact on USA obscenity laws. In the case of Miller,[8] the Chief Justice stated:

> "It is neither realistic nor constitutionally sound to read the First Amendment as requiring that the people of Maine or Mississippi accept public depiction of conduct found tolerable in Las Vegas or New York City."

As Moretti (1984) points out, this adds further to the notion of obscenity as a relative concept:

> "By requiring obscenity to be judged according to the prevailing standards of the community in which the trial takes place, material could be found obscene in one area of the US and not in another."

Public order or private freedom?

It can be argued that, in any civilised society, a balance is required between public order and private freedom. When considering obscene material, there are two key aspects relating to the issue of private freedom. First, the freedom of expression, in that we all have the right to produce what might be considered by others to be pornographic or obscene. Second, the right to privacy, in that one has the right to consume pornographic or obscene material in private. Counteracting the notion of private freedom is the notion of public order. Thus, it can be considered to be the role of the state to ensure that the private freedom of one individual to carry out a certain act does not cause harm, or otherwise impinge upon the rights of another individual. As Williams states (1981):

> "[T]here is a presumption in favour of individual freedom .... what is justifiably curbed by government is only what harms the interests of some citizens."

If one takes the view therefore that all adults have the right to *produce*

---

7   Lord Reid, Knuller v. DPP [1973] A.C. 435, at p457
8   Miller v. California 413 U.S. 15 (1973)

pornography, as part of their freedom of expression, as long as it does not harm or impinge upon the rights of anyone else; then one is likely to see the role of the state and the law as primarily the protector of others, rather than as the prosecutor of the producer. So, for example, the law might focus on those involved in the production of pornography to ensure that their individual rights were not abused. In particular, the law would ensure that children and other vulnerable people are not used in the production of such material.

The *consumption* of pornography and its relationship to individual rights is perhaps more complex. If one maintains the right to consume pornography, one must also equally maintain the right *not* to do so. At its simplest level, this might require the state to prevent obscene material being publicly displayed in inappropriate venues, so that those not wishing to see it can go about their daily business with a guarantee of not having to do so.

It is more difficult, however, for the state to prevent unwanted exposure to obscene material in less public settings – for example, wives being exposed to their husband's use of pornography against their will. If one maintains the argument that such unwanted exposure is harmful, then it follows that it is the proper role of the state to intervene (Williams, 1981). Yet it is difficult to see how the state could effectively police the consumption of obscene material in this way.

The relationship between obscene material and private freedom has been defined in some countries by means of a Bill of Rights. No such written constitution exists in this country. In the USA, the First Amendment states that "Congress shall make no law ..... abridging the freedom of speech or of the press". In its purist form, this would imply that any material, however obscene, cannot be legislated against. As Hunter et al. explain:

> "[T]he regulation of pornography is powerfully inflected by questions of constitutional rights, questions which do not arise in English law .... First Amendment 'absolutists' have been able to insist that it is essential to hold the line against the apparently ever-present danger that governmental and political interests will infringe the individual's fundamental right of free expression in relation to sexual materials." (1993)

Less strict 'absolutists' would accept this general principle, but balance it by allowing the protection of the young and the "unconsenting adult" (Hunter et al. 1993), as discussed above.

Despite the fact that the ruling in Roth[9] took the protection of the

---

9   Roth v. United States 354 U.S. 476 (1957)

Constitution away from obscene material, when the Supreme Court ruled that such publications were without social value, the notion of the freedom of speech within the Constitution still remains as the underlying principle upon which obscenity laws must be based (Moretti, 1984).

The McKinnon and Dworkin ordinance

An alternative way of relating pornography to civil rights was explored by Catherine McKinnon and Andrea Dworkin, two leading American anti-pornography campaigners. In 1983, they drafted an amendment to the Minneapolis Civil Rights Ordinance, which stated that pornography[10] was "a form of discrimination on the basis of sex" and thus infringed ideas of civil rights. The concept behind the ordinance was that women (and children) could claim that direct harm had been caused to them by pornography and pursue a civil action against the producers or distributers of that por-nography. According to the ordinance, civil action could be brought for four reasons: that trafficking in pornography caused discrimination against women; that women had been coerced into pornographic performances; that women had had pornography forced upon them to view; and that women had been assaulted or attacked due to pornography (Dwyer, 1995; Kelly, 1988). Although the ordinance was passed by the Minneapolis City Council, it was finally ruled as 'unconstitutional' by the Supreme Court, meaning that no such law could be passed anywhere in the USA (Kelly, 1988).

To prosecute, censor or classify?

If it is accepted that the State does have a role in legislating against obscene material, a decision then has to be taken about the form such legislation should take. Essentially, there are two main choices – to legislate <u>prior</u> to publication or <u>after</u> publication.[11]

If one opts for the pre-publication alternative, it is most likely to take the form of a classification board. Again, there are two options here. The board can either be allowed to simply *classify* material, be it film or printed matter,

---

10 McKinnon and Dworkin defined pornography as including the following: (i) women are presented dehumanised as sexual objects, things or commodities; or (ii) women are presented as sexual objects who enjoy pain or humiliation; or (iii) women are presented as sexual objects who experience sexual pleasure in being raped; or (iv) women are presented as sexual objects tied up or cut up or mutilated or bruised or physically hurt; or (v) women are presented in postures of sexual submission; or (vi) women's body parts - including but not limited to vaginas, breasts and buttocks - are exhibited, such that women are reduced to those parts; or (vii) women are presented as whores by nature; or (viii) women are presented as being penetrated by objects or animals; or (ix) women are presented in scenarios of degradation, injury, abasement, torture, shown as filthy or inferior, bleeding, bruised, or hurt in a context that makes those conditions sexual.
11 For a full discussion of models of obscenity law enforcement see Dhavan, 1978.

so that no-one can be in any doubt what is being purchased or consumed by referring to the given classification. Alternatively, the classifier can not only be given the power to classify material, but also to censor or, in the most extreme cases, to ban it. In this way, all obscene material available would have a classification marking by which one could judge the level of obscenity contained in it. In either case, the enforcement of the law would focus upon infringements of such classification, including material which has not been submitted to the board prior to publication.

If legislation focuses on dealing with material after it has been published, the judgement about the degree of obscenity present will most likely be made by the courts, according to case law. If it is agreed that the material is obscene, the court will decide what is appropriate and what happens to the material. The alternative way to deal with obscene material after it has been published is to control *where* it is sold or displayed. Infringement to such 'zoning' laws would be the focus of any legislation.

Commissions

One of the ways in which debates have been conducted about obscenity and pornography has been through government commissions or committees. These committees are usually tasked to examine current issues and concerns and to make recommendations about how matters might be improved. This section reports briefly on four of the most important of these commissions: the USA Commission on Obscenity and Pornography (1970); the USA Attorney General's Commission on Pornography (1986); the UK's Williams Committee on Obscenity and Film Censorship (1979); and Canada's Special Committee on Pornography and Prostitution.[12]

The 1970 USA Commission had a budget of $2 million and 19 members, with a full time staff of 11 sociologists, psychologists and lawyers. It "sponsored and financed scores of scientific investigations" (Kutchinsky, 1978). It reviewed the effectiveness of the laws on pornography and obscenity; examined methods of distribution; looked at the effect of pornography on the public and its relation to crime. The report of the Commission concluded that there was:

> "no evidence that exposure to or use of explicit sexual materials plays a significant role in the causation of social or individual harms such as crime, delinquency, sexual or nonsexual deviancy or severe emotional disturbances".

---

12   Only the section dealing with pornography will be discussed.

Consequently, the Commission recommended the repeal of all legislation prohibiting the distribution and sale of sexual material:

> "The Commission believes there is no warrant for continued governmental interference with the full freedom of adults to read, obtain or view whatever such material they wish."

The Commission was concerned with the fact that:

> "much of the 'problem' regarding materials which depict explicit sexual activity stems from the inability or reluctance of people in our society to be open and direct in dealing with sexual matters".

To counteract this, the Commission recommended that the country embark on a grand programme of sex education which would "reduce interest in and dependence upon clandestine and less legitimate sources" of information – i.e. pornography.

All of this proved too much for President Nixon, who rejected the Commission's recommendations out of hand, accusing them of displaying dangerous permissiveness.

The second major US commission reported in 1986. The Meese Commission, as it was known, had a smaller budget than its predecessor ($400,000) and did not conduct any research itself, but rather looked at existing research. The Commission was asked to "determine the nature, extent, and impact on society of pornography in the United States, and to make specific recommendations to the Attorney General concerning more effective ways in which the spread of pornography could be contained, consistent with constitutional guarantees".

In direct contradiction to the previous commission, the Meese Commission found that:

> "The available evidence strongly supports the hypothesis that substantial exposure to sexually violent materials as described here bears a causal relationship to antisocial acts of violence and, for some subgroups, possibly to unlawful acts of sexual violence."

The Commission urged the Attorney General to "direct the United States Attorneys (federal prosecutors) to identify the major sources of obscene material within their districts and commence prosecutions without further delay".

Yet again, the report of the commission had no impact on legislation and was, to say the least, reluctantly received by the Attorney General. Accusations of partisanship on the part of the commission, who were considered by some commentators to be anti-pornography, did not help and the report was dismissed by many as a "sop to the moral right" (Easton, 1994).

In 1977, the Labour government in England set up a similar inquiry, headed by Sir Bernard Williams, a philosopher. The Committee's terms of reference were "to review the laws concerning obscenity, indecency and violence in publications, displays and entertainments in England and Wales ... and to review the arrangements for film censorship ... and to make recommendations".

The Committee recommended the scrapping of existing legislation, to be replaced by a law which "should rest partly upon the basis of harms caused by or involved in the existence of the material .... and partly on the basis of the public's legitimate interest in not being offended by the display and availability of the material". They also recommended a statutory body to conduct film censorship. All other forms of pre-censorship were rejected and instead the Committee advocated restrictions on the display and sale of certain types of material. It recommended that the new provisions would not apply to the written word. It also suggested a new definition of obscenity:

> "[Material which is] offensive to reasonable people by reason of the manner in which it portrays, deals with or relates to violence, cruelty, or horror, or sexual, faecal or urinary functions, or genital functions."

By the time the Committee reported in 1979, there had been a change in government and the new Conservative administration did not agree with its recommendations. No direct changes in legalisation came about as a result of its work.

A special committee in Canada submitted its findings on an examination of "the problems of access to pornography, its effects and what is considered to be pornographic in Canada" in 1985. The views of the Canadian Committee had more in common with the 1970 USA Commission than with Meese. They found that there was insufficient evidence:

> "that pornography is a significant causal factor in the commission of some forms of violent crime, in the sexual abuse of children, or the disintegration of communities and society".

Despite this, the Committee did see a role for the Criminal Code[13] in controlling pornography (Dwyer,1995) and recommended the criminalisation of certain forms of pornography:

> "Because of the seriousness of the impact of this sort of pornography on the fundamental values of Canadians, we are prepared to recommend that the Criminal Code has an important role to play in defining what material may be available in our society."

No direct changes were made to the Criminal Code as a result of the Committee's recommendations, although specific provisions for child pornography introduced in 1993 reflected some of the Committee's concerns.

It can be seen from the above, that commissions and committees appear to have very little direct effect in changing laws on obscenity. This appears to be mainly due to changing political priorities and changing societal attitudes. It is probably not a coincidence that the 1970 USA Commission advocated a "permissive" approach to dealing with pornography during what was considered to be a permissive age; whereas the Meese commission's recommendations reflected a move towards to a "moral religious right" which was apparent throughout the Reagan administration.

What commissions can do is raise the profile of issues such as pornography and encourage debate and argument about them. Such discussions, although not directly responsible for changes in the law, may have a long term impact on the way in which such issues are addressed.

---

13   The criminal Code contains the majority of Canada's criminal law.

3 An overview of laws and controls relating to obscene material in nine countries

This chapter will provide a brief overview of the systems in each country.[1] The following chapter discusses the key characteristics of the various approaches and their implications for controlling obscene material.

Australia

Australia has recently introduced a new piece of legislation – the Commonwealth Classification (Publications, Films and Computer Games) Act 1995 (commenced January 1996). The aim of this Act is to bring together all the various systems of classification under one law and one system. A schedule to the Act contains a National Classification Code to which all Australian State and Territory Governments have agreed to adhere. For this purpose each State has enacted complementary legislation which 'picks up' classification decisions made by the national Classification Board.[2]

While all films, home videotapes and computer games intended for commercial distribution must be classified, only those publications which might fall into the 'Restricted' or 'Refused' categories need be submitted to the Classification Board.[3] The Director of the Board has power under the Act to 'call in' publications considered possibly to fall into those categories. 'Restricted' material in any medium may not legally be made available to persons under 18; 'Refused' material is entirely prohibited and cannot legally

---

1 All countries have specific provisions for the protection of children, these will be discussed in Chapter 4.
2 Sets of classification guidelines for films (including videos), publications and computer games have been endorsed by Censorship Ministers of the Commonwealth and regional jurisdictions for use by the Classification Board.
3 Material is refused classification if it "describes, depicts or otherwise deals with matters such as sex, drug misuse or addiction, crime, cruelty, violence or revolting or abhorrent phenomena in such a way that they offend against the standards of morality, decency or propriety generally accepted by reasonable adults". Refused classification material would include "sexual activity or exploitative nudity of children; promotion, incitement or instructions in matters of crime or violence; bestiality; cruel or dangerous practices – particularly showing apparent harm; sexual violence without consent; promotion, incitement or encouragement of prohibited drugs; exploitative novellas with gratuitous depictions of sexual activity with children, or cruelty or sexual violence without consent."

be disseminated.

The role of the national Classification Board is purely to assign classifications. Enforcement of the law is the responsibility of the States and Territories and prosecutions therefore occur at this, rather than at Commonwealth, level. Prosecutions tend to focus on breaches of classificatory rules. Producing, selling or distributing material which has been refused classification can result in prosecution; as can non-compliance with classifications given – e.g. displaying restricted material outside its classification boundaries or making 'Restricted' material available to minors. Finally, in most jurisdictions, possession of child pornography can also result in a prosecution.[4]

Canada

In Canada the definition of obscenity is contained within the Criminal Code.[5] The definition can be refined through case law and applies to all forms of material – film at cinema, video and publications. The other key control is the Customs Tariff which prohibits the importation of obscene material.

The recent case of R v. Butler[6] defined three different types of pornography: explicit sex with violence, horror or cruelty; explicit sex in which one or more of the participants is degraded or dehumanised; and explicit sex without violence that is neither degrading nor dehumanising. The Supreme Court argued that only the first two of these categories should be subject to restrictions because they will necessarily fail the community standards test of tolerance (Dwyer, 1995).

Cases involving breaches in the law are prosecuted at provincial level as the administration and enforcement of criminal law is a matter which falls under the jurisdiction of provincial attorney generals.

Canada has a classification system for video and films for the cinema, although not for publications. This responsibility presently falls to provincial film review boards but attempts are being made to introduce a national classification system. Such a change would require new legislation.

---

4   The criteria for prohibition contained in the Customs (Prohibited Imports) Regulations reflect those contained in the National Classification Code. Under these regulations, material may be detained by Customs and referred to the Commonwealth Office of Film and Literature Classification for advice as to whether it should be prohibited. If the material is subsequently prohibited, it is forfeited to the Crown. In some circumstances prosecutions may also ensue.
5   The Criminal Code defines obscenity as follows "any publication a dominant characteristic of which is the undue exploitation of sex, or of sex and any one or more of the following subjects, namely, crime, horror, cruelty and violence, shall be deemed to be obscene".
6   R v. Butler, [1992] S.C.R. 452.

England [7]

England's key obscenity law is the Obscene Publications Act 1959. The Act allows for the prosecution of obscene material in two ways. Under Section 2 of the Act, an individual or a company can be prosecuted for a criminal offence.[8] Under Section 3, there is no criminal offence to answer, but rather the power of forfeiture is used which allows the destruction of the seized articles if they are deemed to be obscene by the magistrate. These two processes will often be run in tandem for an individual case.

The British Board of Film Classification (BBFC)[9] is an independent, non-governmental body which, on behalf of local authorities, grants certificates to all films to be shown at the cinema. The right to censor remains with the local authority and it is not unknown, although it is extremely rare, for the local authority to overrule a BBFC decision. The examiners at the BBFC have no written criteria as to what is and what is not acceptable. Their argument for this is:

> "partly because standards shift in line with public opinion, and partly because it is not actually possible to decide in advance what is, or is not, acceptable without reference to a particular context". (BBFC, 1995)

The Video Recordings Act (VRA) 1984 established the BBFC as the designated body in this country for classifying films for release on video. This means the Board has a statutory role for classifying videos but not for classifying films for cinema release. Subsequently, the Criminal Justice and Public Order Act 1994 amended the VRA, confirming the question of harm as the ultimate determinant in the Board's decision making process.[10] The Board can now be held to account for failing to meet the criteria with sufficient rigour.

There is no classification of publications in England.

Northern Ireland relies upon most of the same legislation as England and Wales, with one exception. They prosecute obscene material under the common law offence of obscene libel rather than under the Obscene Publications Act 1959. This means that they do not have a test of obscenity

---

7   This section also applies to Wales and Northern Ireland. Differences in the law in Northern Ireland will be highlighted. However, Scotland will be discussed separately.

8   The offence is triable either-way and can therefore be heard at the magistrates' courts or before a jury at Crown Court if the defendant elects a jury trial or if magistrates decline jurisdiction.

9   It is worth noting again that the original name of this body was the British Board of Film Censors.

10   The amendment, which has become section 4a of the VRA 1984 requires the Board to "have special regard... to any harm that may be caused to potential viewers or, through their behaviour, to society by the manner in which the work deals with: criminal behaviour, illegal drugs, violent behaviour or incidents, horrific behaviour or incidents, or human sexual activity. For the purposes of this section 'potential viewer' means any person (including a child or young person) who is likely to view the video work ... if a classification certificate were issued".

as that material which tends to deprave or corrupt; nor is a defence of artistic merit permitted. Material which is thought to be obscene is seized by the police and put before a magistrate, who makes the decision as to whether or not that material should be forfeited and, possibly, destroyed.

Germany

The legal control of obscene material in Germany is essentially governed by its Penal Code and by the Distribution of Publications harmful to Young Persons Act. The emphasis of the law is focused almost exclusively on the protection of young people. All forms of media are included in these laws.

Germany's Basic Law (Grundgesetz) does not permit any pre-censorship of intellectual property. Thus, by its very nature, the law must rely on prosecuting obscene material after it has been published. However, the Federal Audit Office (FAO) does hold an index of prohibited publications which cannot be sold or distributed to children or young people. The film industry is predominantly self-regulating but there are some statutory restrictions to which they have to adhere.[11]

Prosecutions are carried out by the State prosecutor, for example, for distributing 'indexed' material to young people and selling pornography in inappropriate places. Confiscation and destruction of material is also used.

The Netherlands

The Netherlands has no specific legal controls for classifying or censoring sexually explicit materials. Standards in the country are liberal and freedom of expression is the overriding principle in the constitution. However, the country's Criminal Code does include offences against public morals, the two key aims of which are to protect the public from unexpected exposure to indecent material;[12] and to protect children.[13]

There is a special body for classifying films for cinema release[14] and for broadcasting on television (Nederlandse filmkeuring). Three categories are used: suitable for all ages; suitable for persons over the age of 12; and over

---

11 These statutory regulations restrict the showing of certain films to certain times. Thus, films for children can be shown up to 8.00pm; films for young people under 16 years of age can be shown up to 10.00pm; and films for young people over 16 can be shown up to midnight.
12 This can be either through public exhibition or unrequested mailing of obscene material.
13 Article 240a protects children against the inappropriate displays of pictures or objects which might be harmful to them and Article 240b protects children directly against sexual abuse through their participation in child pornography.
14 The Dutch organisation of video retailers has rules for self-regulating the industry.

the age of 16 respectively. There is only one criteria used when classifying a film – that it might be harmful to young people under 12 or 16 years of age. The classifications are advisory but proprietors of cinemas and broadcasters are bound by the classifications and thus have to display the correct classification and/or not transmit the film on television before a certain time. If an illegal act such as child sex is depicted in the film, action will be taken against the distributors.

Prosecutions are rare and generally aim to fight the production, circulation and public exhibition of child pornography – particularly if there is also evidence of sexual abuse of minors. Priority is given to commercial and professional production and distribution of pornography involving children. In certain circumstances, seizure of obscene material can also occur.

New Zealand

Under the Films, Videos and Publications Act 1993, New Zealand has established a similar system to Australia. The Office of Film and Literature Classification (established with the Act) has a responsibility to classify material into three categories: unrestricted; objectionable;[15] or objectionable dependent upon age of audience, availability and purpose. All forms of media are included with the provisions of the Act. However, only mediums that fall into the category of films[16] must be rated or classified before they are supplied to the public.

Prosecutions can ensue for breaches of classification regulations and for making, distributing or selling 'objectionable' material. It is also an offence to possess 'objectionable' publications.[17]

Republic of Ireland

The Republic of Ireland has a censorship board for publications and a separate censor responsible for films.

---

15 The term objectionable is defined by the 1993 Act as material which "describes, depicts, expresses or otherwise deals with matters such as sex, horror, crime, cruelty or violence in such a manner that the availability of the publication is likely to be injurious to the public good". The Act has detailed and explicit categories for deciding what is 'objectionable' – "a) exploitation of children, or young persons for sexual purposes; or b) the use of violence or coercion to compel any person to participate in, or submit to, sexual conduct; or c) sexual conduct with or upon the body of a dead person; or d) the use of urine or excrement in association with degrading or dehumanising conduct or sexual conduct; or e) bestiality; or f) acts of torture or the infliction of extreme violence or extreme cruelty".

16 The definition of which includes videos and other mediums containing visual images.

17 The Act imposes penalties for supplying restricted publications to persons from whom the Classification Office would restrict them. The Act also empowers the Office to impose display restrictions on the public display of publications.

The Censorship of Publications Board will prohibit material which is "indecent or obscene or advocates the procurement of abortion or miscarriage, or in the case of a periodical publication, that it devotes an unduly large proportion of space to the publication of matter relating to crime".[18] The Publications Board responds to complaints received and to material supplied to them by Customs, rather than systematically classifying all publications.

The Film Censor's Office works in a similar way to the BBFC although it has a legislative base for the classification of both films for cinema release[19] and for video.[20] However, although the Film Censor works closely with the BBFC, he does not necessarily reach the same conclusions. For example, last year the film *Natural Born Killers* was banned in the Republic of Ireland; but a video certificate was given to the film *Mikey* – a decision on which has not yet been reached in the UK. If the distributor of a film disputes the Film Censor's decision, an Appeals Board will meet to reconsider the case.

Scotland

Scotland comes under the jurisdiction of the BBFC for the classification of videos and films for cinema and there is no classification of publications. It has however, a different legislative base to England and Wales for defining what is obscene.

An offence of shamelessly indecent conduct is available under common law which defines obscene material as that which is "liable to create depraved, inordinate and lustful desires in those watching it and to corrupt the morals of the lieges".[21] What is and what is not acceptable is defined by the courts in case law.

The Civic Government (Scotland) Act 1982 created offences of displaying, selling, distributing, printing, and so on of obscene material. There is no new

---

18   This definition has been developed over three Censorship of Publications Acts (1929, 1947 and 1967) and was recently amended by the Health (Family Planning) Act 1979 and by the Regulation of Information (Services outside the State for Termination of Pregnancies) Act 1995.

19   The Censorship of Films Act 1923 states that "the Official Censor shall certify a picture as fit for exhibition in public unless he is of the opinion that it is unfit by reason of being indecent, obscene or blasphemous, or because the exhibition would tend to inculcate principles contrary to public morality or would be otherwise subversive of public morality. In some cases, the Censor may indicate that only part of a picture is unfit for exhibition, and may grant a certificate on removal of that part. The Censor may also grant a limited certificate, restricting viewing to certain classes of person".

20   The Video Recordings Act 1989 states that a video would be unfit for viewing if "the viewing of it would be likely to cause persons to commit crimes, whether by inciting or encouraging them to do so or by indicating or suggesting ways of doing so or of avoiding detection; or the viewing of it would be likely to stir up hatred against a group of persons in the State or elsewhere on account of their race, colour, nationality, religion, ethnic or national origins, membership of the travelling community or sexual orientation; or the viewing of it would tend, by reasons of the inclusion in it of obscene or indecent matter, to deprave or corrupt persons who might view it; or it depicts acts of gross violence or cruelty (including mutilation and torture) towards humans or animals".

21   Watt v. Annan 1978 JC 84, 1978 SLT 198.

definition of obscenity in the Act, so the courts apply the test used in cases of shamelessly indecent conduct – namely whether the material is calculated to deprave and corrupt persons open to depraving or corrupting influences.

USA

The Supreme Court has, over the second half of this century, defined and refined the definition of obscenity.[22] As discussed earlier, the influence of the First Amendment has strengthened arguments against allowing state censorship (and thus a classification system). As Moretti (1984) puts it:

> "Supporters of pornography claim that to again give federal and state governments the power of censorship would inevitably lead to the suppression of constitutionally protected speech and ideas. At bottom, by permitting pornography the courts have chosen the lesser of two evils."

More pragmatically perhaps, it has been realised that, in such a large country both in terms of size and population, it would be impossible to effectively censor or classify the enormous amount of material that would be in circulation at any one time. There is therefore no pre-classification of printed matter.

The film industry operates a voluntary ratings system for film for cinema. The ratings board has no statutory base. Pornography is not normally submitted to the ratings board, but is simply given an 'X' rating by its producers/distributors. A film must be found to be legally obscene to be banned (Moretti, 1984).

---

22 In *Miller* v. *California*, the Supreme Court established a definition of obscenity which still predominates today. It is as follows: "[W]e now confine the permissible scope of such regulation [of obscene materials] to works which depict or describe sexual conduct. That conduct must be specifically defined by the applicable state law, as written or authoritatively construed. A state offense must also be limited to works which, taken as a whole, appeal to the prurient interest in sex, which portray sexual conduct in a patently offensive way, and which, taken as a whole, do not have serious literary, artistic, political, or scientific value". Moretti (1984) suggests that in reality this meant that "the <u>Miller</u> Court was only willing to prohibit 'hard-core' pornography".

4 Discussion

Introduction

As discussed earlier in this report, countries tend to follow a predominantly proactive or reactive approach to controlling obscene material. An emphasis on either one of these approaches will impact on all legislation concerned with regulating such material. This will be apparent in this chapter, which looks in detail at the various types of controls applied to different forms of media;[1] and at the special provisions for child pornography.

Those countries whose legislation focuses on the proactive classification of obscene material tend to have quite rigid definitions of the sorts of material that should be regulated. For example, as outlined in the previous section, both Australia and New Zealand have produced detailed criteria that must be taken into account when classifying material. The alternative approach, adopted by the UK and the USA, is to allow the definition of obscenity to develop over time, through case law. Such an approach requires a vaguer definition of obscenity which can be interpreted and re-interpreted by the courts.

It can be argued that a rigid definition of obscenity allows for a more objective and simple assessment of material. It is a relatively straightforward process to refer to a list of activities and behaviours, check for their occurrence in the material and make a decision based on whether or not they appear. There is little scope for personal views to influence decisions and therefore a degree of consistency in defining obscene material should be achieved.

Using case law to define obscenity is a more complex process which must take into account perhaps contradictory judgements made over a long period of time, none of which might be strictly relevant to the present material. This approach is, by its very nature, more subjective and, therefore, more open to the prejudices and personal biases of those making the

---

1   Controls concerned with obscenity on television are not included. In all the countries encompassed in the review, including the UK, such controls are almost entirely separate from those related to film, video or written publications and do not come under the jurisdiction of the criminal law. Indeed, countries which do operate any controls over what is shown on television do so generally through self-censorship and regulation by the television companies themselves. The nine o'clock watershed in this country is an obvious example of such regulations. The state's role in such controls is, at the most, marginal.

judgements. It does however more readily allow for flexible decision making which can reflect current standards in society and adapt over time to any changes in those standards.

Cinema

The majority of countries have some form of classification and/or censorship of films prior to their release at the cinema. Some systems operate on a voluntary basis, working with the film industry, establishing the criteria with which they work over time and with experience; others work within a specific piece of legislation which outlines the criteria upon which their decisions must be made. The former model is that which is favoured by the BBFC; the latter by the Office of Film and Literature Classification (OFLC) in Australia.

The OFLC would classify a film as an 'M' (Mature – suitable for audiences aged 15 years and over) if it contained the following:

"Most adult themes may be dealt with, though the degree of explicitness and intensity of treatment will be an important factor.

Language: Crude language may be used, but not if overly frequent or impactful.

Sex: Sexual intercourse or other sexual activity may be discreetly implied.

Violence: Realistic violence of low intensity may be depicted if contextually justified.

Other: Drug use may be discreetly depicted, but not in an advocatory manner. Supernatural and 'horror' special effects may be depicted, but not if graphic or impactful."

The BBFC works with the same age category – 15 – but does not have written guidelines as to what might be included in a film. Examiners look for similar factors when making their decisions – nudity, sex, violence, horror etc. – but there are no hard and fast rules about what can and cannot be included. As mentioned above, the main argument for the BBFC's system is that it allows current standards to be taken into account in any decisions reached. It also allows for a judgement to be made about the context in which any image is depicted, so that nothing is ruled out simply on the basis of it being included on an 'outlawed' list. So, for example, a film which chronicles a story of incest might be passed if the story was told responsibly.

Such a system can, however, make it difficult to know why a particular film is classified in one way, when another, similar film, is given a higher or lower classification. Yet again, it appears that a degree of subjectivity can creep into the decision-making process. This is not necessarily problematic, as experienced examiners may have very good reasons, based on their specialised knowledge, for classifying two similar films differently. However, without written standardised criteria, it is not always possible to know explicitly whether the judgements made are fair and it is possible to argue that, for example, current moral panics in the media, might have undue influence on the final decision. With the Australian system, one can more readily see why a film is given a certain category and therefore one can make an easier judgement as to whether the film is appropriate viewing for, say, one's own children. Nevertheless, a more rigid system, whilst permitting some scope for interpretation, does not allow so readily for current standards and the context of the narrative to be taken into account.

The BBFC is currently attempting to address the problem of balancing a contextually-based approach with the need for public scrutiny of their decision-making. They believe that one way of alleviating some of the difficulty might be to provide consumer advice that summarises the issues involved and are presently negotiating with the video industry about the most effective way of providing such advice.

Some countries have national classification boards. Others have local boards, so that the standards which are implied can be given a local interpretation.[2] For example, Canada has provincial film boards with responsibility for classifying movies. Local boards can be useful if there are regional sensitivities or difficulties which need to be borne in mind – for example, the murder of a local child – when classifying a particular film. However, such local systems may also allow for the prejudices of a small number of people to overly influence what is made available to the community.

Video

In some countries, the viewing of films on video is seen as conceptually different to viewing films at the cinema and, as a result, different criteria are applied when controlling material on video. The reasons for this are that, first, films on video can be re-wound, fast-forwarded and freeze-framed, allowing a more concentrated and de-contextualised viewing of the images; and, second, there is no official gate-keeper, such as the box office at the

---

2   In the UK, the judgement of the BBFC can be overruled by Local Authorities, allowing some local influence on their decision-making.

cinema, to prevent children and other vulnerable people seeing inappropriate material.[3]

Such concerns are reflected in legislation in the UK, the Republic of Ireland and Germany, all of whom apply stricter criteria for classifying videos than for films at the cinema. In all three countries, films previously classified for cinema release have to be re-submitted prior to their release on video and may receive a stricter classification or require cuts before receiving the same classification.

In the UK, as outlined earlier, the VRA 1984 gave the BBFC a statutory basis upon which to classify videos, something they do not have for classifying films for cinema release. This legislation requires that the BBFC considers all "potential viewers" for the video – notwithstanding the age classification the film is likely to receive. The Board has to bear in mind that children may see '18' films at home and therefore has to consider if any harm might come to them from watching a particular film.[4] A similar system is used in the Republic of Ireland although they do not necessarily reach the same conclusions as the BBFC.

The protection of young people is also the focus of the German video classification system. Unlike films for cinema release, videos are defined as "printed matter" and therefore come under the jurisdiction of the FAO indexing system described earlier. Videos which are classified as '18' may be indexed by the FAO and consequently will "be subjected to severe promotional and distribution restrictions" (The European Video Directory, 1995) aimed at protecting young people from exposure to the material.

Australia and New Zealand do not have stricter criteria for video than they do for films for cinema release. It might be argued that their more rigid classification system and use of detailed consumer advice renders such additional legislation unnecessary.[5] However, their systems cannot take into account the differing experiences of watching films at the cinema or on video.

Printed material

Of all the media, the control of obscene printed material appears to be the

---

3 Of course, many would argue that this is the job of parents and guardians.
4 In making their assessments, the BBFC take into account two key aspects of the film – *address* (which would include such things as subject matter, manner of depiction, use of language and so on); and *appeal* (use of well-known stars, potential marketing etc.). This might mean, for example, that a film starring Arnold Schwarzenegger might be cut more heavily for violence because of his great appeal to teenagers and, therefore, the likelihood of the film being seen by them.
5 As mentioned earlier, the BBFC is attempting to introduce a voluntary system of providing more detailed consumer advice on videos.

most difficult and results in the widest variety of arrangements between the countries included in the review.

Some of the countries make no attempt to classify or censor printed material prior to publication (UK, Germany, Canada and USA). These countries generally rely on the seizure and prosecution of such material under obscenity laws – which, if successful, would result in its destruction. The law is again dependent upon case law to define whether or not the material is obscene. In Germany, printed material is indexed in the same way as video (see above).

One of the key arguments for not having any pre-classification of printed matter is simply that, given the volume of material produced, it would be an extremely costly and time-consuming process. This problem is also acknowledged by those countries which do attempt to operate a pre-publication classification system. For example, in Australia, no attempt is made to classify every publication in circulation in the way films for the cinema are classified. Only those publications that are likely to exceed the guidelines for 'unrestricted' publications or are considered to lie on borders of the 'unrestricted/restricted' categories are required to be submitted for classification.[6] Publishers may submit publications on a voluntary basis or the OFLC can require them to submit for classification any publication considered to fall within the definition of a "submittable publication".[7] Such publications can be brought to the notice of the OFLC by complaints or as a result of their own enquiries. In practical terms the vast majority of material is self assessed by the industry. As a safeguard, any contentious material can be classified prior to release and this service is used by prudent operators in the industry.

Similarly, in the Republic of Ireland, the Censorship of Publications Board (CPB) relies upon complaints from the public or upon material being drawn to their attention by customs officials and does not have a systematic procedure for classifying printed material. However, that is not to say that the CPB is not active. Sixteen publications were banned in the latter half of 1995, including two newspapers (*Ireland's Daily Sport incorporating Daily Sport* and *Ireland's Weekend Sport incorporating Sunday Sport*).

Realistically such systems are unlikely to capture anything like the real market in printed material. However, it can be argued that having such a

---

6   The categories for publications are Unrestricted (which can be sold anywhere); Restricted – category 1 (which have to be sold in opaque wrappings); Restricted - category 2 (which have to be sold from specific outlets); and Refused Classification (which are entirely prohibited). There are some differences in the ways in which the various states use this legislation. For example, Queensland does not recognise the two Restricted categories and material falling into these groups would be refused classification in that state.

7   According to the 1995 Act, "submittable publication" means an unclassified publication that, having regard to the Code and the classification guidelines to the extent that they relate to publications, contains depictions or descriptions of sexual matters, drugs, nudity or violence that are likely to cause offence to a reasonable adult to the extent that the publication should not be sold as an unrestricted publication.

classificatory system at least allows the prosecution of such material to be more straightforward. The Australian OFLC can classify forfeited material, which has not previously been submitted, making the court's job somewhat easier.

Child pornography and the protection of children

One of the key roles of any obscenity legislation is to protect young people – both as potential consumers of such material; and also as potential participants in the production of pornography. As discussed earlier, many countries deem that adults have the right to consume whatever material they wish provided vulnerable people, and particularly children, are sufficiently protected from being exposed from harmful images. For example, the Australian OFLC states in its documentation:

> "Adults in a free society should be allowed as far as possible to see what they wish, and creative artists, including film-makers, to depict what they please without fear of intervention by the State. It is generally accepted, however, that the exercise of these rights carries certain responsibilities and must be subject to a number of constraints for the good of society as a whole. Our right to see what we please cannot be allowed to infringe the rights of others. Children and young people, in particular, must be adequately protected from material likely to harm or disturb them…"

The concern to protect young people is reflected in specific legislation in many countries. Such legislation can be placed in two groups – that concerned with child pornography and that concerned with child protection – although the two are obviously not mutually exclusive.

In England, the Protection of Children Act 1978 prohibits the taking, distributing and possession, with a view to distribution, of indecent photographs of children.[8] Two points are worth noting here. The possession of such photographs can be an offence and the test is not one of obscenity but of indecency, which is considered to be simpler to apply (and, consequently, to prove). Penalties are severe. A person convicted on indictment of possession (with a view to distribution) of indecent photographs of children can be sentenced to up to three years imprisonment and an unlimited

---

8   The Act was amended by the CJPO Act 1994 to include 'pseudo-photographs' which would include, for example, images of children created on computer. The Civic Government (Scotland) Act 1982 includes similar provisions. It is also worth noting that, under the Criminal Justice Act 1988, it is a summary offence to possess an indecent photograph of a child under the age of 16. The maximum penalty for this offence is six months in prison and a £5,000 fine. This became an imprisonable offence following an amendment in the CJPO Act 1995.

fine. Similarly, in Canada, the Criminal Code contains separate statutory pro-hibitions for child pornography, with severe penalties even for possession.

Every jurisdiction included in the review incorporates in its definition of obscenity, or in its classification code, specific categories concerned with the sexual imagery of children. Again, the tests are usually more straight-forward than those related to adult material, in that a 'straightforward' picture of a naked child could be sufficient to result in a prosecution (or material being prohibited). Similarly, in the USA, the Supreme Court[9] ruled that material containing child sex did not have to be ruled obscene in order to be prohibited, nor did any defence of public good have to be applied. This ruling gave states the power to prohibit any material depicting child sex – including possibly scientific and artistic material (Moretti, 1984).

In The Netherlands, which might be considered to have the most liberal laws, the protection of young people is nevertheless considered to be very important. However, unlike some other countries, only material which depicts children participating in sexual behaviour is illegal; a nude photograph of a child for example, taken by its parents at home would not be considered indecent or obscene.

Germany's obscenity laws are focused almost exclusively on the protection of young people – through its Distribution of Publications harmful to Young Persons Act. All laws relating to the display, distribution and sale of obscene material are specifically concerned with protecting children and young people from being exposed to such material. The index of obscene material maintained by the FAO (discussed above) comprises that material which is considered to be harmful specifically to young persons. In this country, the VRA 1984 was also specifically concerned with children being exposed to harmful videos in the home. Similarly, in The Netherlands, it is a criminal offence to supply material to minors which might be considered harmful.

It can be seen therefore that, regardless of way in which countries control obscene material overall, all take very seriously the protection of children and young people from such images. Many would argue that this is where the true role of the state lies (see for example, Robertson, 1979 and Williams, 1981).

---

9   New York v. Ferber, 458 U.S. 747 (1982).

Indecent displays and postal restrictions

The countries included in this review were not asked specifically about either the display or the mailing of indecent or obscene material. It is therefore beyond the scope of this paper to discuss this issue in detail. However, it should be noted that restrictions do apply to these practices[10] and, indeed, there are often stricter regulations concerning what can be considered to be unwelcome intrusions into people's private lives. So, for example, unsolicited 'mailshots' containing indecent[11] material are often prohibited; as are public displays of obscene material, particularly where children might be exposed to them.

---

10   In this country the Indecent Displays (Control) Act 1981 and the Post Office Act 1953 apply.
11   Note that the lesser test of indecent rather than obscene applies to material sent through the post in this country.

4 Conclusion

Controlling obscene material has always been, and undoubtedly always will be, a problematic area of the law. A topic which so frequently evokes such an emotional, subjective and individual response does not make any easy subject for state control. As Robertson says:

"English obscenity law may be illogical in theory, uncertain in scope, and unworkable in operation, but few nations have discovered any satisfactory alternative ... The problem of obscenity is intractable and does not by its very nature admit of a legal solution which will satisfy everyone." (Robertson, 1979)

This report did not aim to offer simple solutions to the complex problem of legislating against obscene material; but rather aimed to highlight possible approaches for doing so – some of which might be more successful than others, but none of which present a wholly satisfactory answer.

However, before one even begins to look at different possible approaches, one first must decide what it is that the law should prohibit and who it should protect. For example, should the law focus on banning only that material which features images of sex with children or sexually violent material? Or should all sexually explicit material be subject to state control? And should the law focus exclusively on protecting children from exposure to and/or involvement in pornography? Or is it the duty of the state to protect everyone from such 'harmful' influences?

The countries included in the review offered different answers to these questions. Canadian law clearly states that non-violent sexually explicit material which is neither degrading or dehumanising should not be subjected to prohibition. The USA and the UK, with their vaguer definitions of obscenity, make no such distinctions; and although, in reality, one would not expect such material to be prosecuted, there is nothing to clearly state that it could not be.

Of all the countries included, Germany's focus on the protection of children and young people is the most explicit. However, most countries saw this as a particular area for concern and this was reflected in specific legislation. The degree of freedom allowed to adults to consume obscene or pornographic material varied too. Those countries with a bill of rights or written constitution appeared to more readily accept that adults should be free to see whatever material they wish, but usually with the caveat that their actions did not harm others. Those countries without such constitutions did not appear to be so heavily influenced by arguments about individual freedom.

The choice between proactive and reactive options for controlling obscene material represented the most obvious differences between the countries. What was less obvious was which approach was more effective. Proactive controls, chiefly taking the form of classification, appeared to offer a high degree of consistency in dealing with obscene material. Reactive controls, mainly relying on the judgements of the courts, offered more flexibility and thus perhaps more readily could reflect changing attitudes in society. Perhaps most obviously, a combination of the two approaches might be the best solution. One would however have to bear in mind that some media, i.e. cinema and video, lend themselves more readily to classification; whereas others, i.e. printed matter, do not. Most countries appeared to have recognised this to some extent and much of the classification work carried out was restricted to film for cinema and, more recently, to video too. Such work is also directly linked to the protection of children and young people, a key area of concern as already highlighted.

One thing is certain. The future is going to present more difficulties. With new technologies come new ways to present and consume obscene material. Cable and satellite television, computer games and the Internet are obvious examples. None of these media lends itself readily to controls and, whilst the law is attempting to keep pace, it is faced with a considerable challenge.

References

Attorney General's Commission on Pornography (1986) *Final Report.* Washington DC. US Government Printing Office.

British Board of Film Classification. *Annual Report 1994-95.* London: BBFC.

Brophy, S. (1977) *Screen Violence and Film Censorship.* Home Office Research Study No.40. London: HMSO.

Dhavan, R. and Davies, C. (1978) *Censorship and Obscenity.* London: Martin Robertson.

Dhavan, R. (1978) "Existing and alternative models of obscenity law enforcement". in **Dhavan, R. and Davies, C.** (eds.) *Censorship and Obscenity.* London: Martin Robertson.

Dwyer, S. (1995) *The Problem of Pornography.* California: Wadsworth.

Easton, S.M. (1994) *The Problem of Pornography: regulation and the right to free speech.* London: Routledge.

European Video Directory (1995).

Eysenck, H. J. (1978) "Psychology and Obscenity: a factual look at some of the problems." in **Dhavan, R. and Davies, C.** (eds.) *Censorship and Obscenity.* London: Martin Robertson.

Howitt, D. and Cumberbatch, G. (1990) *Pornography: impacts and influences.* London: Home Office Research and Planning Unit Occasional Paper.

Hunter, I., Saunders, D. and Williamson, D. (1993) *On Pornography: literature, sexuality and obscenity law.* London: Macmillan Press.

Itzin, C. (ed.) (1992) *Pornography: women, violence and civil liberties.* Oxford: Oxford University Press.

Kelly, L. (1988) "The US ordinances; censorship or radical law reform?" in **Chester, G. and Dickey, J.** (eds.) *Feminism and Censorship: the current debate.* Dorset: Prism Press.

Kutchinsky, B. (1978) "Pornography in Denmark – a general survey" in **Dhavan, R. and Davies, C.** (eds.) *Censorship and Obscenity.* London: Martin Robertson.

MacMillan, P. R. (1983) *Censorship and Public Morality.* Aldershot: Gower.

Mathews, T. D. (1995) *Censored: the story of film censorship in Britain.* London: Chatto and Windus.

Moretti, D. S. (1984) *Obscenity and Pornography: the law under the first amendment.* New York: Oceana Publications.

Newburn, T. (1992) *Permission and Regulation: law and morals in post-war Britain.* London: Routledge.

Newnham, D. and Townsend, C. *"Pictures of Innocence"* The Guardian Weekend, January 13 1996.

Phelps, G. (1975) *Film Censorship.* London: Victor Gollancz.

Report of the Special Committee on Pornography and Prostitution. (1985) *Pornography and Prostitution in Canada*: Volume 1.

Robertson, G. (1979) *Obscenity: an account of censorship laws and their enforcement in England and Wales.* London: Weidenfeld and Nicolson.

Rolph, C. H. (1961) *The Trial of Lady Chatterley.* London: Penguin.

Trevelyan, J. (1978) "Film Censorship and the Law" in Dhavan, R. and Davies, C. (eds.) *Censorship and Obscenity.* London: Martin Robertson.

United States Commission on Obscenity and Pornography. (1970) *Report of the Commission on Obscenity and Pornography.* Washington DC: US Government Printing Office.

Williams, B. (1981) *Obscenity and Film Censorship: an abridgement of the Williams report.* Cambridge: Cambridge University Press.

Publications

List of research publications

A list of research reports for the last three years is provided below. A **full** list of publications is available on request from the Research and Statistics Directorate Information and Publications Group.

Home Office Research Studies (HORS)

130. **Car theft: the offender's perspective.** Roy Light, Claire Nee and Helen Ingham. 1993. x + 89pp. (0 11 341069 7).

131. **Housing, Community and Crime: The Impact of the Priority Estates Project.** Janet Foster and Timothy Hope with assistance from Lizanne Dowds and Mike Sutton. 1993. xi + 118pp. (0 11 341078 6).

132. **The 1992 British Crime Survey.** Pat Mayhew, Natalie Aye Maung and Catriona Mirrlees-Black. 1993. xiii + 206pp. (0 11 341094 8).

133. **Intensive Probation in England and Wales: an evaluation.** George Mair, Charles Lloyd, Claire Nee and Rae Sibbett. 1994. xiv + 143pp. (0 11 341114 6).

134. **Contacts between Police and Public: findings from the 1992 British Crime Survey.** Wesley G Skogan. 1995. ix + 93pp. (0 11 341115 4).

135. **Policing low-level disorder: Police use of Section 5 of the Public Order Act 1986.** David Brown and Tom Ellis. 1994. ix + 69pp. (0 11 341116 2).

136. **Explaining reconviction rates: A critical analysis.** Charles Lloyd, George Mair and Mike Hough. 1995. xiv + 103pp. (0 11 341117 0).

137. **Case Screening by the Crown Prosecution Service: How and why cases are terminated.** Debbie Crisp and David Moxon. 1995. viii + 66pp. (0 11 341137 5).

138. **Public Interest Case Assessment Schemes.** Debbie Crisp, Claire Whittaker and Jessica Harris. 1995. x + 58pp. (0 11 341139 1).

139. **Policing domestic violence in the 1990s.** Sharon Grace. 1995. x + 74pp. (0 11 341140 5).

140. **Young people, victimisation and the police: British Crime Survey findings on experiences and attitudes of 12 to 15 year olds.** Natalie Aye Maung. 1995. xii + 140pp. (0 11 341150 2).

141. **The Settlement of refugees in Britain.** Jenny Carey-Wood, Karen Duke, Valerie Karn and Tony Marshall. 1995. xii + 133pp. (0 11 341145 6).

142. **Vietnamese Refugees since 1982.** Karen Duke and Tony Marshall. 1995. x + 62pp. (0 11 341147 2).

143. **The Parish Special Constables Scheme.** Peter Southgate, Tom Bucke and Carole Byron. 1995. x + 59pp. (1 85893 458 3).

144. **Measuring the Satisfaction of the Courts with the Probation Service.** Chris May. 1995. x + 76pp. (1 85893 483 4).

145. **Young people and crime.** John Graham and Benjamin Bowling. 1995. xv + 142pp. (1 85893 551 2).

146. **Crime against retail and manufacturing premises: findings from the 1994 Commercial Victimisation Survey.** Catriona Mirrlees-Black and Alec Ross. 1995. xi + 110pp. (1 85893 554 7).

147. **Anxiety about crime: findings from the 1994 British Crime Survey.** Michael Hough. 1995. viii + 92pp. (1 85893 553 9).

148. **The ILPS Methadone Prescribing Project.** Rae Sibbitt. 1996. viii + 69pp. (1 85893 485 0).

149. **To scare straight or educate? The British experience of day visits to prison for young people.** Charles Lloyd. 1996. xi + 60pp. (1 85893 570 9).

150. **Predicting reoffending for Discretionary Conditional Release.** John B Copas, Peter Marshall and Roger Tarling. 1996. vii + 49pp. (1 85893 576 8).

151. **Drug misuse declared: results of the 1994 British Crime Survey.** Malcom Ramsay and Andrew Percy. 1996. xv + 131pp. (1 85893 628 4).

152. **An Evaluation of the Introduction and Operation of the Youth Court.** David O'Mahony and Kevin Haines. 1996. viii + 70pp. (1 85893 579 2).

153. **Fitting supervision to offenders: assessment and allocation decisions in the Probation Service.** Ros Burnett. 1996. xi + 99pp. (1 85893 599 7).

Research and Planning Unit Papers (RPUP)

72. **The National Probation Survey 1990.** Chris May. 1993.

73. **Public satisfaction with police services.** Peter Southgate and Debbie Crisp. 1993.

74. **Disqualification from driving: an effective penalty?** Catriona Mirrlees-Black. 1993.

75. **Detention under the Prevention of Terrorism (Temporary Provisions) Act 1989: Access to legal advice and outside contact.** David Brown. 1993.

76. **Panel assessment schemes for mentally disordered offenders.** Carol Hedderman. 1993.

77. **Cash-limiting the probation service: a case study in resource allocation.** Simon Field and Mike Hough. 1993.

78. **The probation response to drug misuse.** Claire Nee and Rae Sibbitt. 1993.

79 **Approval of rifle and target shooting clubs: the effects of the new and revised criteria.** John Martin Corkery. 1993.

80. **The long-term needs of victims: a review of the literature.** Tim Newburn. 1993.

81. **The welfare needs of unconvicted prisoners.** Diane Caddle and Sheila White. 1994.

82. **Racially motivated crime: a British Crime Survey analysis.** Natalie Aye Maung and Catriona Mirrlees-Black. 1994.

83. **Mathematical models for forecasting Passport demand.** Andy Jones and John MacLeod. 1994.

84. **The theft of firearms**. John Corkery. 1994.

85. **Equal opportunities and the Fire Service.** Tom Bucke. 1994.

86. **Drug Education Amongst Teenagers: a 1992 British Crime Survey Analysis**. Lizanne Dowds and Judith Redfern. 1995.

87. **Group 4 Prisoner Escort Service: a survey of customer satisfaction.** Claire Nee. 1994.

88. **Special Considerations: Issues for the Management and Organisation of the Volunteer Police.** Catriona Mirrlees-Black and Carole Byron. 1995.

89. **Self-reported drug misuse in England and Wales: findings from the 1992 British Crime Survey.** Joy Mott and Catriona Mirrlees-Black. 1995.

90. **Improving bail decisions: the bail process project, phase 1.** John Burrows, Paul Henderson and Patricia Morgan. 1995.

91. **Practitioners' views of the Criminal Justice Act: a survey of criminal justice agencies.** George Mair and Chris May. 1995.

92. **Obscene, threatening and other troublesome telephone calls to women in England and Wales: 1982-1992.** Wendy Buck, Michael Chatterton and Ken Pease. 1995.

93. **A survey of the prisoner escort and custody service provided by Group 4 and by Securicor Custodial Services.** Diane Caddle. 1995.

Research Findings

1. **Magistrates' court or Crown Court? Mode of trial decisions and their impact on sentencing.** Carol Hedderman and David Moxon. 1992.

2. **Surveying crime: findings from the 1992 British Crime Survey.** Pat Mayhew and Natalie Aye Maung. 1992.

3.   **Car Theft: the offenders' perspective.** Claire Nee. 1993.

4.   **The National Prison Survey 1991: main findings.** Roy Walmsley, Liz Howard and Sheila White. 1993.

5.   **Changing the Code: Police detention under the revised PACE codes of practice.** David Brown, Tom Ellis and Karen Larcombe. 1993.

6.   **Rifle and pistol target shooting clubs: The effects of new approval criteria.** John M. Corkery. 1993.

7.   **Self-reported drug misuse in England and Wales. Main findings from the 1992 British Crime Survey.** Joy Mott and Catriona Mirrlees-Black. 1993.

8.   **Findings from the International Crime Survey.** Pat Mayhew. 1994.

9   **Fear of Crime: Findings from the 1992 British Crime Survey.** Catriona Mirrlees-Black and Natalie Aye Maung. 1994.

10.   **Does the Criminal Justice system treat men and women differently?** Carol Hedderman and Mike Hough. 1994.

11.   **Participation in Neighbourhood Watch: Findings from the 1992 British Crime Survey.** Lizanne Dowds and Pat Mayhew. 1994.

12.   **Explaining Reconviction Rates: A Critical Analysis.** Charles Lloyd, George Mair and Mike Hough. 1995.

13.   **Equal opportunities and the Fire Service.** Tom Bucke. 1994.

14.   **Trends in Crime: Findings from the 1994 British Crime Survey.** Pat Mayhew, Catriona Mirrlees-Black and Natalie Aye Maung. 1994.

15.   **Intensive Probation in England and Wales: an evaluation.** George Mair, Charles Lloyd, Claire Nee and Rae Sibbitt. 1995.

16.   **The settlement of refugees in Britain.** Jenny Carey-Wood, Karen Duke, Valerie Karn and Tony Marshall. 1995.

17.   **Young people, victimisation and the police: British Crime Survey findings on experiences and attitudes of 12 to 15 year olds.** Natalie Aye Maung.

18. **Vietnamese Refugees since 1982.** Karen Duke and Tony Marshall. 1995.

19. **Supervision of Restricted Patients in the Community.** Suzanne Dell and Adrian Grounds. 1995.

20. **Videotaping children's evidence: an evaluation.** Graham Davies, Clare Wilson, Rebecca Mitchell and John Milsom. 1995.

21. **The mentally disordered and the police.** Graham Robertson, Richard Pearson and Robert Gibb. 1995.

22. **Preparing records of taped interviews.** Andrew Hooke and Jim Knox. 1995.

23. **Obscene, threatening and other troublesome telephone calls to women: Findings from the British Crime Survey.** Wendy Buck, Michael Chatterton and Ken Pease. 1995.

24. **Young people and crime.** John Graham and Ben Bowling. 1995.

25. **Anxiety about crime: Findings from the 1994 British Crime Survey.** Michael Hough. 1995.

26. **Crime against retail premises in 1993.** Catriona Mirrlees-Black and Alec Ross. 1995.

27. **Crime against manufacturing premises in 1993.** Catriona Mirrlees-Black and Alec Ross. 1995.

28. **Policing and the public: findings from the 1994 British Crime Survey.** Tom Bucke. 1995.

29. **The Child Witness Pack – An Evaluation.** Joyce Plotnikoff and Richard Woolfson. 1995.

30. **To scare straight or educate? The British experience of day visits to prison for young people.** Charles Lloyd. 1996.

31. **The ADT drug treatment programme at HMP Downview – a preliminary evaluation.** Elaine Player and Carol Martin. 1996.

32. **Wolds remand prison – an evaluation.** Keith Bottomley, Adrian James, Emma Clare and Alison Liebling. 1996.

33. **Drug misuse declared: results of the 1994 British Crime Survey.** Malcolm Ramsay and Andrew Percy. 1996.

34. **Crack cocaine and drugs-crime careers.** Howard Parker and Tim Bottomley. 1996.

35. **Imprisonment for fine default.** David Moxon and Claire Whittaker. 1996.

36. **Fine impositions and enforcement following the Criminal Justice Act 1993.** Elizabeth Charman, Bryan Gibson, Terry Honess and Rod Morgan. 1996.

Research Bulletin

The Research Bulletin is published twice each year and contains short articles on recent research.

Occasional Papers

Employment opportunities for offenders. David Downes. 1993.

Sex offenders: a framework for the evaluation of community-based treatment. Mary Barker and Rod Morgan. 1993.

Suicide attempts and self-injury in male prisons. Alison Liebling and Helen Krarup. 1993.

Measurement of caseload weightings associated with the Children Act. Richard J. Gadsden and Graham J. Worsdale. 1994. (Available from the RSD Information and Publications Group).

Managing difficult prisoners: The Lincoln and Hull special units. Professor Keith Bottomley, Professor Norman Jepson, Mr Kenneth Elliott and Dr Jeremy Coid. 1994. (Available from the RSD Information and Publications Group).

The Nacro diversion initiative for mentally disturbed offenders: an account and an evaluation. Home Office, NACRO and Mental Health Foundation. 1994. (Available from the RSD Information and Publications Group).

Probation Motor Projects in England and Wales. J P Martin and Douglas Martin. 1994.

Community-based treatment of sex offenders: an evaluation of seven treatment programmes. R Beckett, A Beech, D Fisher and A S Fordham. 1994.

Videotaping children's evidence: an evaluation. Graham Davies, Clare Wilson, Rebecca Mitchell and John Milsom. 1995.

Managing the needs of female prisoners. Allison Morris, Chris Wilkinson, Andrea Tisi, Jane Woodrow and Ann Rockley. 1995.

Local information points for volunteers. Michael Locke, Nick Richards, Lorraine Down, Jon Griffiths and Roger Worgan. 1995.

Mental disorder in remand prisoners. Anthony Maden, Caecilia J. A. Taylor, Deborah Brooke and John Gunn. 1996.

An evaluation of prison work and training. Frances Simon and Claire Corbett. 1996.

Books

Analysing Offending. Data, Models and Interpretations. Roger Tarling. 1993. viii + 203pp. (0 11 341080 8).

Requests for Publications

Home Office Research Studies from 143 onwards, *Research and Planning Unit Papers, Research Findings and Research Bulletins* are available **subject to availability** on request from:

Research and Statistics Directorate
Information and Publications Group
Room 1308, Home Office
Apollo House
36 Wellesley Road
Croydon CR9 3RR
Telephone: 0181 760 8340
Fascimile: 0181 760 8364
Internet: http/www.open.gov.u/home_off/rsdhome.htm
E-mail: rsd.ha apollo @ gtnet.gov.u.

Occasional Papers can be purchased from:
Home Office
Publications Unit
50 Queen Anne's Gate
London SW1H 9AT
Telephone: 0171 273 2302

Home Office Research Studies prior to 143 can be purchased from:

HMSO Publications Centre

(Mail, fax and telephone orders only)
PO Box 276, London SW8 5DT
Telephone orders: 0171-873 9090
General enquiries: 0171-873 0011
(queuing system in operation for both numbers)
Fax orders: 0171-873 8200

*And also from **HMSO Bookshops***